This book is for

Bud and Judy,
James Andrew McEvoy,
and, of course, Anne Murray

snatch

judy macinnes jr.

ANVIL PRESS
VANCOUVER

Snatch

Copyright © 2000 by Judy MacInnes Jr.

All rights reserved. No part of this book may be reproduced by any means without the prior written permission of the publisher, with the exception of brief passages in reviews. Any request for photocopying or other reprographic copying of any part of this book must be directed in writing to the Canadian Copyright Licensing Agency (CANCOPY) One Yonge Street, Suite 1900, Toronto, Ontario, Canada, M5E 1E5.

Printed and bound in Canada
First Edition
Cover design: Rayola Graphic Design
Author photo: J. Andrew McEvoy

CANADIAN CATALOGUING IN PUBLICATION DATA

MacInnes, Judy 1970–
Snatch

Poems
ISBN 1-895636-27-2

I. Title
PS8575.I5284S62 2000   C811'.54   C00-910043-1
PR9199.3.M322S62 2000

Represented in Canada by the Literary Press Group
Distributed by General Distribution Services

Anvil Press
Suite 204-A 175 East Broadway,
Vancouver, B.C. V5T 1W2   CANADA

Contents

Horizontal Iceberg / 9

Cinema Self / 10

Jellyfish Child / 11

Bird Land / 13

Jill Started Shaving / 15

Super Socco Story / 17

Southern Accents / 18

Digging into the Smooth / 19

Do You Want to Buy My Sister? She's Really Cheap / 20

Begging for Cookies / 21

Jean Fox & Debbie / 22

Little French Maid / 23

Children Who Look Like Ice Cream / 25

Clinking Glasses / 26

Frog Legs & Perfume / 27

Pretend Mole / 28

Scotch Mints / 29

Chalk Outline / 30

Clichéd Super Socco Stories / 31

Brown Car Story / 32

Something Round / 34

Small Penis Poems / 35

Shimmering Strip / 36

Luv Junket / 37

Even Outside / 39

Examination / 40

Pump Fish / 41

Potato Peeler / 44

The Colour of Your Choice / 45

Four of Everything / 47

How Do Snake Handlers Fall in Love? / 49

Chaos Theory / 53

Stagette / 55

Hairdo Lady / 56

Running Amber / 58

Cross-section of an Ex's Brain / 60

I Love Doing My Wife / 61

Sundress / 62

This Normal Morning / 64

Probe / 65

Imagine A Stranger / 66

Taffy / 67

Chaff / 68

Terminology / 70

America's Funniest Home Videos / 72

Tiny Bat / 73

Better Homes, Better Gardens / 75

Happy Days Motor Inn / 77

Deadpan / 78

Fertility Window / 79

Troll / 80

Manjeet / 82

Blue Grandma / 83

Prayer for Her Future Husband / 84

Accident / 94

Lure / 96

Acknowledgements

About the author

Horizontal Iceberg

Two nights ago I skated
the Beaufort Sea, hunting
for the perfect vagina
in ice. A hole so diamond
cut and cold, its insides
furnished with saws, it could easily
divide an innocent man
in half. Like magic, icebergs
swelled and when I woke up
I hated poetry.

With eighty-three percent of my body
under the covers, I knew
something very dangerous had happened
during the night.

Cinema Self

Kick-ass boots, black leather
pants, purple sweater (cowl
necked), chunky silver
jewellery, 5'11", long
hair past my ass, 110 pounds and tan,
driving a gold TransAm, perfect
hairless legs, king-size bed with an ocean view,
white cotton sleepware, opening a great handbag,
searching for smokes, pills, an address, in that
order.

Jellyfish Child

My big sister says I was made
in water
during the summer of '72
while our parents were vacationing
in Florida.

Dad released himself
in the Atlantic Ocean, opening,
closing like a giant umbrella, and Mum
happened to be dog-paddling by.

Four hundred tiny eggs nested
between her toes, armpits and legs
until she wiped them off
and joined Dad for cocktails in the hotel lounge.

In dreams, I'm drifting
in thick salt water
trying to attach myself to

rock beds, coral,
an open clam shell.

You're a jellyfish child,
my sister insists
a clear circle,
a plastic bag
       floating
on the surface.

Bird Land

Surrey isn't a one way street, isn't finger bowls, isn't
Wagner, isn't ethereal, R.E.M. sleep, or double entendre.
Isn't grain elevators, Kerrisdale, or the P.N.E. Surrey
isn't the Eiffel Tower, in vogue, film noir, or a palindrome.
Isn't high-rises, or area code (416). Isn't Red Zinger tea,
isn't raison d'etre, isn't iguana, immaculate, or spats. Surrey
isn't yoga, or yogurt. Isn't Steveston, abbreviations, or
Abbotsford. Isn't one of the Seven Natural Wonders of the
World. Isn't marlin fishing, isn't Commercial Drive, or
continental drift. Isn't Constantinople, Costa Rica, Coventry,
or Cyprus. Surrey is a commonly misspelled word.

Surrey is a swizzle stick. Is drive-ins and teen pregnancy.
Ditches, slugs, expansion. Surrey is a posthypnotic
suggestion, is cutting classes, Big Macs, and abduction.
Surrey is Walley Exchange, public pools, salt and pepper
shakers, the YMCA. Is high beams and fog lights. Is
mushroom farms and crisis lines, pawn shops and strip
malls. Surrey is between Hope and Burnaby. Surrey is

hopscotch, freeway entrances, dogwoods. Is vivisection, abortion clinics, cream soda, and hard candy. Surrey is pancake breakfasts, the Rodeo, parking lots. Surrey is worse than Esquimalt. Is minimum wage. Surrey is two dozen roadways named after birds. Canary Drive, Flamingo Avenue, Peacock Lane,

Swallow Circle.

Jill Started Shaving

In grade six
Jill started shaving her
arms from wrist
to elbow
with a yellow Bic.

I plucked
my eyelashes
one
by
one
mistaking them
for eyebrows
hundreds of brown crescent moons
curled in the sink.

Debbie dipped Q-tips in Nair,
delicately cleaned
her nostrils.

Pammy yanked fistfuls of baby
fine hair from the crown
of her head.

At the school assembly
rules about hair removal were
enforced. There was to be no more
sleep-overs. Girl Guide meetings were cancelled.

Even then it was never considered safe
for girls to be alone
in washrooms together.

Super Socco Story

My mom and I are in the grocery store and I'm begging her for two litres of Super Socco, the Drink*of*Champions. She's hesitating because groceries go so fast in the house, what with my sisters being such pigs and all. Anyway, we're up at the check-out, and she's like, *Okay, okay, get the goddamn Super Socco,* and I'm running through the meat section, past the wieners, past the bean and pasta section, and finally, I grab it, and it's glowing with a perfect radiance. Three days go by but nobody's touched it. It's after school and I've locked myself inside because there's some maniac snatching kids in the neighbourhood. When I finally look outside I see two girls running across our yard, trying to jump the fence. So I open the door and invite them in and fill two glasses so high with Super Socco it spills on the coffee table and I don't even think about tasting it.

Southern Accents

Rolanda Lynn Dinwoodie and I started walking to school together in grade six right after Pammy Chung and Debbie Palmieri dumped me. They said I was becoming too critical and controlling. I missed school for a week I was so sick. On our way to school Rolanda and I would eat our lunches and the best part was when we'd suck back juice and stomp on the boxes, screaming, *Help, help, police. I've been shot,* in southern accents.

Digging into the Smooth

Mum holds a big glass bowl of lemon Jell-o over our heads like a nineteen-fifties housewife exhibiting a freshly baked apple pie so the apple and crust smell wafts in the kitchen like a domestic perfume. Before my sisters, my Dad, and I help ourselves to yellow, we say, *Digging into the smooth.*

Do You Want To Buy My Sister? She's Really Cheap

I'm fourteen and I need Bonne Belle Lip Smacker. I collect my valuables (five gold chains, pinky ring, mood ring, silver earrings from Mexico, a chunk of jade, nickels circa 1935), take the public bus for the second time in my life, and go to Rusty's Pawn and Gun Shop on the King George Highway. I pretend to browse, then uncover my goods. Rusty tells me to go home and look for something bigger.

Begging for Cookies

I don't know how Rolanda knows this, but if you walk up certain driveways and slowly knock on the door, put your hand out like you're waiting for a low-five, you are given cookies. Without having to say a word. How do they know what she wants?

For years, I thought there were psychics in her cul-de-sac.

Jean Fox & Debbie

My sisters were hacking around Heath Elementary smoking and they found this dog and brought her home and they asked me what to call it. *Jean Fox, Jean Fox,* I called. A little brown mutt of a dog, affectionate as hell. One day, like all things, Jean Fox, that stray dog who wormed her way into our hearts, died. She did not die in my arms like Tinker. No, not Jean Fox. She died in the wild. Didn't hear until recently that she had been shot in the guts with a B.B. gun because she was into the neighbour's chickens.

One night, at Debbie's house, we were all drinking and her brother walks in and goes, *Sheeba's dead*.

Little French Maid

When I fall deep in love, I make a clucking sound. Runs in my family. First heard it from Granny, my Grandma's mom, who used to sleep a lot, and cluck to me after her breakfast. Every morning Grandma would go in Granny's room and take away the plate, the spoon, the Royal Dalton teacup. Then you heard it. A cluck. Clear as a bell. A little demand. Granny wanted me to jump on her bed and keep her alert as she said the rosary. *Hail, Mary.*

When I fall deep in love, I make a clucking sound. Order my man around. Keep him on his toes. Now I understand why my three older sisters costumed me when I was four years old. They would come home from high school, turn on *Family Feud*, and cluck. I would enter, aproned and high-heeled, carrying a note pad, pencil poised. I would speak with my head down. I would say, *What do you please, Master? What do you please?* Giant illegible loops (their orders for the kitchen) filled paper.

There's this little hollow part in the mouth when you cluck that makes love come and fill beauty in.

Children Who Look Like Ice Cream

Dorrit Dinwoodie used to sew her daughter outfits for special occasions: birthday parties, class outings, Valentine's Day. On picture day, Rolanda Dinwoodie would be in pigtails. The world somehow depended on this. If you like, you could say that the sun rose and set in those pigtails. In grade three, on that October morning when our class was to be photographed, Pammy Chung noticed. *You look like ice cream, Rolanda.* And she did. Like French ice cream, pink and white and brown and pigtailed. A parfait, frappe, dessert.

Clinking Glasses

Why is there this need to show other people you're happy and having fun when you're alone? Sometimes after school, my parents at work, my sisters out driving the Malibu, I'd spread the curtains just enough for you to see my hands clinking wine glasses together for a toast.

Frog Legs & Perfume

I start off small, spritzing a light breezy mist of Mum's cologne, *L'Temps*, walk into it like she does. A dab behind the ears. Another quick spritz on the lamp shade. A couple of sprays behind my right shoulder for luck, or is it the left one? Then something inside me snaps. In my room, I spray posters — HANG IN THERE, SKI BUMS, KISS ME QUICK, ONE NUCLEAR BOMB CAN RUIN YOUR WHOLE DAY, and the one with the kid dumping a bowl of spaghetti on his head — inch by square inch, until they're wet and dripping, moaning with perfume, pooling in the shag carpet. A colossal Scratch 'n Sniff Experience.

The migraine starts in my eyes. I pass out on Gravol. The dream is about a boy who finds a thousand frogs, chops off their legs, delicacy.

Pretend Mole

My big sister used to say that if someone ever stole one of us girls and replaced us with an impostor, she would be able to know us by our moles. Katrina Rose with her mole under her ear. Terri with a perfect new moon on her wrist. Mine, on my left elbow.

Every morning before Dorrit Dinwoodie goes to work at the school cafeteria, she dots a mole on her cheek with an eyebrow pencil. She touches it up at recess. Climbing up the stairs to Rolanda's room, I notice her parents sleep in separate bedrooms.

Scotch Mints

Rolanda Lynn and I were lying on my three-quarter bed sucking on scotch mints until she started choking, and then I stepped in, wrapped my arms around her stomach (our first hug), and pulled hard enough for the candy to pop out of her mouth so she could put it back in and start sucking again.

Chalk Outline

Rolanda Lynn Dinwoodie's favourite subject was Art because she could draw anything without tracing (bald eagles, grinning seahorses, Garfield). Her pipe cleaner and popsicle stick collection was, in a word, *Impressive.* She was the only one of us who refused to lie down on those black sheets of construction paper so the teacher could outline our bodies.

Our silhouettes so fine, so gritty, like the salt you find around fancy glasses, fierce red drink.

Clichéd Super Socco Stories

David and I exchange stories in the dark. I ask him if he wants to hear some family baggage. He pauses and says, *Yeah, tell me.* I tell him this: my maternal grandmother, who died four years ago, married her brother-in-law. I pause, mimicking his own pauses, his moments of contemplation. Then he tells me this: his grandparents on his father's side were kicked out of a retirement village in Florida because they were drinking heavily, smoking in their room, and swearing in the lounge. They were sent back to Winnipeg to dry out. After we stop laughing and after a long silence, he tells me how he buried a world map and a box of Ritz crackers in his backyard when he was a kid. *What a clichéd Super Socco Story, Dave,* I say, with some displeasure. And then without missing a beat he says, *My life is filled with them.*

I think about all the stories that bury things, twinkling on the pages, like stars.

Brown Car Story

I just got off the phone with Gina Vanderberg. During our conversation I told her, *You know the brown car Grandpa gave me when I was sweet sixteen, no stopping me, our entire grade jealous because they wanted the 4-door wonder, that brown piece of chocolate velvet, incredible love machine, Oh, how I've kissed boys in that car, windows up, incense burning, the places I've seen, Tofino, Portland, Kelowna, endless trips through car washes, running red lights, smiling my way out of tickets, faded dashboard, fuzzy dice, the morning I went to a gas station and the attendant insisted on washing the inside of the windshield, the memories, all the memories, California or bust, my first accident, my first flat tire, recharging the battery? So I sold it a couple of months ago, told the chick who insisted on buying it that it was old and tired with memories. I told her, 'Hey, that's okay if you can't give me a hundred bucks for it right now but when I need the money, I'll just ask for it.' And now since I don't have a job, $42 in the bank, I wrote her and said, 'Hey, how about* *that money?' She phones me later, says, 'I drove that brown car around for a month and then I took it from Victoria to Vancouver and then I drove it around some more and then I took it to get safety inspected and the guy told me that I'd have to pay a junk dealer to get it off my hands.' So I say to her, 'What are you trying to tell me?' She tells me everything again, says she doesn't have the car anymore, it's parked somewhere in Vancouver, doesn't want to pay me for it. Then I told her, 'I need to think about this. Let me call you back.'*

I'm no longer on the phone with Gina. This story isn't finished. I'll get opinions from my family and friends, try to explain how big and lonely Vancouver is.

Something Round

She wanted something
she couldn't have. Something to get
her hands around, the fur
of pubic hair, a muff, a simple
protection, a four-month
pregnancy. She wanted the luxury
of travelling eggs before
her seventh birthday. She wanted
to give birth on the top bunk before
she started menstruating. She wanted something
hot to the touch, baby rhinestones, a ticket,
a name change, the sensation
of a blow-fish expanding in fear.

Small Penis Poems

1.
We're both eight
and my cousin from San Diego climbs
me, his cold arms grip
my legs, the tip
of his tiny penis

2.
Mom holds Grandpa
up in the tub while I circle
knee with face-cloth

3.
It's groundhog day;
there's nothing for me
to get my mouth around, his penis
tunnels, digging
into itself

Shimmering Strip

The first time he admits seeing her naked, he compares her thighs to sliced pears. Describes them as thick and wet, ready for serving, piled high on softening ice. A smorgasbord set for the universe.

She thinks *Mirage*, thinks travelling all day, searching out a telephone, to call for a tow, to lift her off her back.

But they are at his sister's house, in the guest bedroom, a view of the Fraser, only place to be alone. Listening to disco under bedclothes, chink of ice, pools sapping, he becomes a dew worm picker, on his knees, relentless, picking everything out of her in a puddle, laughing at the way it goes in, easy.

Luv Junket

oh baby call me your little steak-bite any time follow me
around like those groupies travelling in the hundreds
gathered at the ninth hole waiting for the perfect swing ah
the ninth hole I love the way you say that love finding
socks curled between your KING-SIZE box-springs keeping
away our sounds oh yes as embarrassing as sugar butter
sandwiches could live off the stuff and you too baby can
never be the same after you've done what you've done
turning me inside out like a kid's T-shirt skin a rabbit
stripping down at the laundromat washing pots frying pan
sizzle then letting me down on telephones you don't even
know the number of next thing you know you're two-step
strutting up King George Highway in your favourite corduroy
shirt singing *When the Saints Go Marching In* while thinking
of me in bed buying tiger lilies and pies at B.B. Bakery
three blocks out of your way bumping into each other at
Woodwards sucking back bulk honey swerving across the aisle
gunning for my hips surprising me in the meat section
laughing at the wieners tight against the cellophane taste

it baby taste sweet on my pinky ring and we're getting down
on flecked linoleum kicking kicking us out I Just Wanted
Pork Chops Mister you don't have to be so rude and jealous
oh baby show me teeth flash tongue eat these from my hands
pearl onions a turnip small candy I'd steal anything for
you it's Thanksgiving at the vacant lot where we stop a
grunion run delicacy dreaming Nancy Drew picking out
dragonflies from the rest scooping out luv junket cream.

Even Outside

things smell like us! We buy breakfast at Farmer's Market —
sweet oranges, honey tangerines, out-of-season grapes —
break bundles of bananas apart because we only need two.
Our fingers, like tent-flaps, stretch out, holding on to
giant grapefruits. Little boys strolling to elementary school
wiggle their small teeth at us. Even in the Chinese Bakery,
breads are glazed and wet!

Examination

I thought
it was truly scientific between us.
A deliberate
dissection of lust.

The only way
I could see inside of him
was to make several incisions;
fold, pin the skins back;
separate gall bladder,
kidney, spleen.

He was an easy catch, rising
up from the water,
Deus Ex Machina, dumb.
As if he were riding
an escalator to the centre
of my bedroom.

Pump Fish

When your boyfriend presses his palms and fingers, flat and hard as two-by-fours, down on your chest, you remember the fish at Link Lake, the summer you turned ten. His hands seem to be working on you, trying to revive you like a paramedic would. A few minutes earlier, you were sure he was checking for a pulse. And when he moves from the bed, to the window, to the dresser and back to the window again, you remember how your father circled the campground, trailer full of daughters, looking for a spot to spend the night. You counted, *Four, five, six*, each time the car, hauling the rented trailer, passed the woodpile, *seven, eight*, while your cousin, Michael, sat up front between your parents. It was twelve bucks a night for the site he finally picked next to the bathrooms and close to a swing-set your sisters said they were too old to play on. Poplars blocked your family's view of the highway. Your boyfriend comes back to you, stands beside the bed for a moment, covers your legs with the bedspread, and for the fifth time tonight braces himself against the dresser. Your father did his best to circle indoors, too. Pushed himself past paper plates, smoking mosquito coils, buckets of chicken, slouching clotheslines, spinning around the broken zipper of your sleeping bag while your mother rested after a full day of travelling. Now it's your boyfriend who holds your feet at the end of the bed. After dinner, your sisters, flashlights tucked into back pockets, took off down to the lake, leaving you to watch Michael fill the tires of his bicycle. You think your father told you to leave the campsite, find your sisters, urged you to do something other than stare into space. So you followed your cousin to a different part of Link Lake where certain birds could be mistaken for your eldest sister's laughter. Your boyfriend, still in the room, waits for you to respond to his mouth, his fingers, his face. Like Michael's when he reached a point in the path where he could see a wooden dock and a boy jigging for fish. An intense face, quick, ready to please. You took the line when the boy was called for supper and jerked on the string as instructed. You imagined your father, underwater, circling the bait. Ready to snap. And tonight you imagine your boyfriend, all fingers, pulling a line. As soon as Michael took over, a green and grey fish, with fins as fat as cigarette butts, jumped, hooking itself. You remember the fish dying and gasping, your fingers poking, Michael's hands cupping the fish out of water. You remember him running back to the campsite and placing the damp fish evenly down on a stone the size of a man's hand. You tried to smooth the fish out while he found a twig near the fire pit, propped the gills open, shoved the bike pump in its mouth, pushed down on the handle.

But on other nights, your boyfriend is like the fish out of water because like a child, like a poem, he starts inside of you. And you push and breathe into his mouth like that bike pump until you hear the sounds of his lips opening, the warm water, the struggle in his voice.

Potato Peeler

Your ex, with the vegetable body, would take off when you and the guys from the bar yelled in her green pepper ears, *Keep your eyes peeled, Mary.* She feared utensils that could strip away the skin. And when you tell me enough of your past, I imagine her driving away in your Buick with thoughts of eyes. Translucent strips of membrane, carrot clippings, brown wrappings of an onion, hairy skins of peaches tossed into a heap of compost. I'm not surprised when you say, unfastening my bra with one hand, I'm getting under your skin, or to see Mary, who is now jogging by, finally fall. Beet red knees raw and pared.

The Colour of Your Choice

You used to paint anger green and large on onion skin
sheets. Onions, you told me once, are bitten like apples by
brown children in warm places. Green and large, these
pictures, matted with dark squares: you at eight, fighting
and rolling on the lawn with a neighbour, yards of pulled
hair snarled with grass. Grass, you breathe, the colour of
frantic ivy. And I see one ivy plant waiting near our bed:
twisted and wet, like your simple arm behind my bare legs
and back and when my body shifts, moving blankets, sheets;
you shake and toss like an embarrassed lawn mower in a
garden cemetery. Fine sheets, with the taste of our skin.
My legs open too wide for you sometimes. I can't seem to
feel you anymore. But I feel the sheets on my legs, tangled
around my shoulders, and that is you. You paint anger with
your tongue now. It flounders in my mouth: a thick chalk
stain. Still green. I sit waiting, wrapped in beads and
tissues: posing. Draw me like those wooden women with
drooping necklines, who like to hide with scarves. They are
natural and carved, you told me once. Don't forget to paint

me. I have licked your brushes moist in mouth, dipped my legs into the colour of your choice, outlined my body on paper.

Four of Everything

Walking along racks of used wool suits in St. Vincent de Paul's, pinstriped, single-breasted, lapels, I tell my girlfriend that I'm past my prime because the women in my family find their men when they're under ninety pounds. Dad could wrap his big hands around Mom's waist, squeeze her into a slippery oval shape, until his fingertips touched one another. When my girlfriend left her husband, I took her to get her ears pierced. She eventually went back to him. This time, when my guy says it's over, she takes me to buy old-fashioned evening gowns that we will cut so short they will be stylish. There are so many things here, four of everything, luxury, selection! We are reminded of our big grandmothers, a time when people owned standing ashtrays, and how love can still be found in objects.

And I know there are other fish in the sea. And I know there is more than fish in the sea. And I know about the boy from West Vancouver who jumped off a cruise ship on its way to Florida. We are so lucky! I would be an idiot to compare him, leaving his shoes and glasses on deck, to you leaving me again. I will never dream of loss, like that boy's mother, opened up and gliding on the backs of dolphins.

How Do Snake Handlers Fall in Love?

1.
This is the egg tooth.
Cutting ways out of a shell.
Dropping from the snout of an indigo snake days after birth.

Reminding her of the difficulties of escape.

Between games of gin rummy, she knives mango flesh, stacks orange pieces around piling cards, erects miniature stone fences. He takes and eats, then offers the last fruit slice to her. They haven't known each other for long, just a few sentences. But we already know she'll win every hand. She has a fruit cutter's precision, a card player's quick fingers. Possibly after her defeat, he'll suggest a bath, pour water, undress her in the hallway, bite his lip as she steps into the tub. When they are comfortable, he'll spread her legs, move a razor down her shins like he's known her body for years. It is at this invented moment, when we've pictured two lovers shaving each other, that he sees the appendix scar on her belly. Lower right. Should we be comparing this mark to a bow in a clothesline? A wrinkle? The first slit in the snake's egg shell?

2.
This is the snake jaw.
Working like a double-jointed hinge.
Swallowing frogs whole and headfirst.

Reminding him how things walk prey down their mouths.

Clutching deep brown bags, the lovers search for indigos, glide their way through deep gorges, sycamores, creeks of catfish, like a snake might. It's past noon so they huddle underneath stands of yellow birch to unload cheese and a thermos from his knapsack. She fiddles with her bra strap, while he cuts food into strips on a flat rock. Has this hunt for blue skins, through the West Virginia Mountains, really made them hungry? This time, she initiates the undressing, pulls her shorts down by the thumbs, toes the creek bed, draws his body inside water.

3.
This is the shedding.
Sidewinding against gravel to loosen old skin.
Peeling off like a rented wetsuit.

Reminding them of difficult escape.

He captures two diamondbacks while she rests on the rock face. Here, her dreams move in the same pattern as the trapped rattlers: recoiling, sliding, struggling. Recently, he visits her sleep, chases her through apartment buildings; into gravel pits; along grain elevators; finally grabbing her behind the head to charm and handle her until morning. Because her body is now in the shade, she wakes to pull on a sweater. Shouldn't they have found the snakes together? During the car ride back into town, through dirt roads and railway crossings, her right arm dangles out of the passenger window. These lovers want to become reliable for us, like the rows of wedding dresses in Liberty's One Hour Dry Cleaning. But we're wondering what his dreams were like before knowing her. Without the desert boa, trapped against artificial rock in Ben's World Famous Circus Store, would they have captured each other at all?

Chaos Theory

Chuck buys baguette and brie. Blond, blue-
eyed. Fairly tall. Twenty-
five years old. Conceived
at a K.O.A. Kampsite, twelve miles south
of Mt. Rushmore, South Dakota.
No siblings. Likes
hiking, reading. Generally avoids eye
contact. Slips and falls
on the tiles outside Uprising Bakery.

Debbie jogs by. Black hair. Brown eyes.
Child Care Worker. Libra. Same
demographic. Notices Chuck
fall, offers assistance. She knows first aid
but will still break
his heart.

Debbie initiates a general conversation
about slugs. Chuck adds, *A slug's heart
will continue to beat when removed*

from the body. He gives Debbie his phone number. She's flattered. Everything seems innocent but develops into a routine.

Stagette

Surprise! Doubles of everything: toaster ovens,
salad spinners, woks, even the male stripper
brings a twin! The Mother of the Bride, tipsy
on Peach Champagne, concentrates,
staples bows and ribbons onto a paper plate.
We wrap the bride-to-be in toilet paper — little mummy —
a doll inside a doll inside another. We play
The Memory Game. On a tray, an ear plug. Chop
stick, cuff link. *Remember what is placed
in front of you.* Saucer, twist tie,
feather. *Remember what you serve.* Choker,
pot holder, eraser. *Remember the little things
that might come in handy.* Eyebrow tweezers, coaster,
teething ring. *Remember who you are before
you become someone else.*

Hairdo Lady

Hairdo Lady! Hi, I'm Hairdo Lady. What hairdo can I do for you today, Lady? I say

and he's going, *Hey, today, I'm the Hairdo Lady. Hair-Do-Lay-Day. It's the day for doing hair!*

Really, it's a hooker, split ends down to her ass, trotting the street. And really, it's the morning, and we're all late for work.

Lady, Lady.... Hairdo Lady. She's Hell On Wheels. She's Long Gone.

After we lived together for five months he said, *You're just like me. You repeat nonsensical phrases over and over!*

Miami! Miami! Budda-Budda-Bing! Budda-Bing!

There are people that are made for you.
There are people you can be yourself around.

Hey Big Fella. Big Spenda.

When Mum phones she says, *When's the wedding? Why buy the milk when you can get the horse for free?*

Budda-Bing! Miami!

Last night, my pick, he cooked European wieners on our new BBQ, made coleslaw. I laid back, watched TV, called to him from the living room, said, *Mum? When's dinna, din-din dinna, gonna be, gonna be, Red-Dee?*

Running Amber

Ever since the blast at 16347 Cormorant Lane, Alan considered his favourite nephew, Gary, to be the target for bad luck. But Gary's luck really began to turn sour at the age of seven when he sprouted from 3'11" to a staggering 5'4". Naturally, Gary's classmates worshipped him, and, at first, began doing small favours for him, like giving him extra sandwiches and picking him at least second for sports teams. The prestige ended all too soon when, at the bitter age of eight, Gary stopped growing. Some blamed it on vertigo. Others, the transmitter his father kept in the basement. Others blamed themselves entirely.

The night of the blast, Gary had become bored. Alan and his live-in girlfriend Shelly were on the porch pickling vegetables from their garden. Automobiles, warm and stuffy on the main drag, ran ambers and honked. Hoods steamed outside Johnny's Supper Club. Gary merely stepped onto the gravel driveway, inducing a chemical reaction.

All the Racing-Car-Red nailpolish on Shelly's feet and

hands exploded off. A pound and a half of cucumbers ended up three city blocks away, interrupting a stagette in full gear, where Steamy La Beefe insisted he would never jump out of a cake again. Plenty were scared. And everybody agreed whatever Gary had inside him that made him stop growing was powerful enough to destroy anything.

Cross-Section of an Ex's Brain

Stealing induces passion
so when we shimmied past the hostess in Pizza Hut
without paying our bill, why didn't you want to screw
in our getaway mini-van like teenage criminals?

How about a peck on the cheek for running
the red?

I don't care if Ann Landers thinks it's dangerous
to share our fantasies.

As we sped home to catch *Sports Page*
I imagined the cross-section of your brain,
fairly blank, lined with ovals and cells,
X's and O's, a simple play designed
to eat up the clock.

I Love Doing My Wife

I am an elderly man with a young wife. We have a puppy, a baby son. I am the owner of new shoes. None of these things seemed to have existed prior to this moment. I read the paper in the morning with awe, thinking, *Look at all I still don't know. Look how the world changes. Look at how everything grows to become new again.*

I am old. The blisters on my feet are the newest additions to my body. I love having sex with my wife. Everything in the garage can be thrown out. Sometimes I discard objects I don't own. Green garbage bags containing clothes, small appliances still in boxes, books, collectible records line the side of our house. Sally Ann is doing a pick-up. I love doing my wife.

I take the puppy around the block. She stands, immobilized, too young to walk on a leash, I carry her home, bundled in my overcoat, imagine myself, heart-attacked, falling down onto the gravel driveway.

I love my wife. I'm returning the shoes.

Sundress

Nothing of any real importance happened that day.

I stood in the bathroom. Held a towel against my body like a sundress. Held the towel against myself like a sundress, over my sundress. Nobody was around. Nothing of any real importance happened that day. The bathroom was out of toilet paper. Nothing left. When I stood in the tub with my clothes on, I heard her on the telephone through the heat register making *The Final Arrangements.* I wore two sundresses that day. Outside, through the milked bathroom window, I noticed that nothing of any real importance happened. A long rectangular car with a foreign motor, crunched down on gravel. *Rang,* the telephone, *rang, rang.* Flower arrangements began arriving. The door connecting the bathroom and the master bedroom was noticeably open. She answered the door and pointed them to the bedroom. The two men, *from the car?*, strolled in. Closed the door so she couldn't see. Two men dressed in dark blue uniforms entered. Their jackets had zippered fronts. Zippered to their necks. Nothing of any real importance happened that day. I stood on the closed toilet seat, hunched over, and mouthed, *I'm still in here. Don't start what you're doing while I'm here.* But, like folding clean sheets, the twins, only a few seconds separating them, shook the bag loose. The bag was big enough to fit a person. Nothing of real importance. I was in the adjoining bathroom. Two guys walked in, didn't notice the sundress I was wearing, covered Grandpa with a plastic three-piece suit.

This Normal Morning

we wait for the windowwasher to finish our side of the condo. The fact our home is sealed off this way unnerves you. Already dressed, you lean against the door, middle of your forehead pressed against the peephole. Was it only she, with a bucket of detergent and a squeegee, who prevented us from sleeping an hour more? Was she the only reason why we hurriedly drove up a street we didn't even want to be on? Paired like ambulance drivers making our way to a foreign scene, we rolled down the windows, in rhythm with a siren.

Probe

It is difficult to understand what your brother tries to tell you at first, drunk, in your parent's living room. It reminds you how it used to be, Mum and Dad in Palm Springs, leaving you to fend for yourselves, several weeks at a time. During their absences, you both pretended they were dead, drew the curtains, stopped answering the phone, ate Cream of Wheat, drank Mailbu Rum, played strip poker round the clock. But you're trying to forget about the past surrounded by moving boxes, and in times of danger, like this time, you speak about your spouses to remind yourselves you are both adults now. At first you laugh when he reveals himself to you, tells you Julie, his secret mouse of a wife, was abducted by aliens when she was a teenager. The aliens descended on her in the form of a fireball. Since the abduction and subsequent return, he confides, she is terrified of fire. Suddenly you understand. Fire roars in the living room, it is so incredibly hot when you take off your clothes, deal up the cards.

Imagine a Stranger

,a hairy, well-built man, making love to your wife. You know people like that exist, a man or a woman willing to fill the shoes of another, much like a stunt double taking over if a scene proves too dangerous. You imagine him hunkering down on her, thick come pouring out of him — *well, if you have to verbalize it* — like a caulking gun. He does a pretty good job screwing her but not as good as you. You see this man as an extension of yourself and you get off watching him, not your wife. This could be your double. We are told everybody has one.

Taffy

An acquaintance of yours is a qualified taxidermist. Ten years ago, over-tired, needing a loan, crying in your beer, you promised to send him future business — your mum's lap dog — if he could only help you out, this one last time. Since this promise, your friend has moved a thousand miles away, has set up a small shop across the street from the House of Mystery and inquires monthly about Taffy's health.

You cannot sleep because when you dream, you dream violence.

Taffy, on her haunches, unbalanced, like a standing bear, chases after you. You feel the dream in your hands and understand why, in almost every language on earth, the word for mother begins with an M sound. When you teach your children to play ball, you lose your cool, *You want to know how you throw, Kid? You throw bad.* Even after Taffy's body is found in the train wreck, you're sure everyone thinks you're an asshole.

Chaff

Before I stepped one steel toe into this place, I dreamed metal spouts reaching like arms across the Distributor Floor, orange gates fixed on the cleaners, shafts, and brooms. Dan, over first coffee break, tells me the best part of sleep is the last five minutes because you dream about landscapes you've never seen before. Turn a day of cylinders and slabs into sunsets.

Usually I'm posted as a sweeper but tonight I'm watching grain go by on a black rubber belt thicker than my wrist. Checking every fifteen minutes for a mix. Nothing more impossible to separate, in the known universe, than barley and wheat.

I watch for eight hours until it disappears into Three Receiver, slugs up Eight Leg, shoots onto the Transfer Belt, out to the boat. During second break I stay in my own shack, flip through the paper. Glance at the horoscope. Check scores.

Watching flax go by, I grab a coffee can's worth, slowly sift it through the screen, knowing this moving flax travels more miles in three weeks than I ever will. I wonder about that last part of dreaming.

Terminology

We didn't
understand
    one another
so I pointed
    to what
hurt me, not
on my own body
    small of back,
    nape of neck — but
on the Doctor Doll,
a shaped piece of ivory,
elephant
tusk, illegal
and white: a reclining woman
with parts and
plasma smoothed
over.
Six centimetres long,
the size of a human

foetus not quite
formed, toes and
fingers shaped
like
paws.

America's Funniest Home Videos

The toddler is caught.
A bean bag chair sliced open;
guts on the playroom floor.

Her mother, frantic.
The camcorder is dead.

Silly Boo, she snaps, *Stay put
til I get the other battery.*

Boo waits in an inch of beans,
orange Exacto knife cradled
in her tiny fist.

Tiny Bat

The iron plugged in and upright, even though
one side of her little party dress is still wrinkled.
My daughter is crying in her room.

I open her door, disoriented because
she has rearranged the furniture again.
The bookcase now huddled in the alcove,
Mum's old desk with a sewing machine
tucked in its belly faces the window.
She's sprawled on her three-quarter bed
newly placed against the wall.
I pet her hair, her hunched back.
She smells like Tiger Balm.

The carpet needs vacuuming.

I recall Mum lugging the burgundy sectional
across the hardwood floor every time
Dad left.

My daughter squints at the light coming
from the hallway, wraps her arm around her head
like a tiny bat. I ask
what's wrong, offer her tea
and toast until she nods.

In the kitchen, I hear her moving things. I burn
a whole loaf of bread before bringing the tray upstairs.

Better Homes, Better Gardens

Dad's attracted to abandoned cabins, climbs
cat ladders to roof cladding, construes
meaning from the condition of shingles. Even
on Gabriola Island, a place where he has come
to spend two weeks with me, something inside
of him, perhaps a magnet behind his eyes, draws him
to deserted homes to figure their past.

She left him for someone else, he says, patting
his palm against the faint numbers
on the mailbox. He checks for mail, nods when
he finds the box empty. *Yup, Buddy was left high
and dry. See that overlap and the way
the chimney leans to the left?*

It all happens in his mind. The empty
mailbox. The day the owner's wife left Gabriola,
her fingernails splitting as she pulled a green
garbage bag of laundry to the pickup.
He sees what used to be garden. A metal shed

in the distance, secured with a thick lock.
Faded flannel sheet strung across
the window for a curtain. Imagines a phone call
before supper, potatoes burning pots black, her final
stride out the door. Dogwood chopped
and stacked at the side of the house. Green moss
spreading like poster paint on stucco. The hose, coiled,
hangs on the chain link fence like
a decorative wreath.

I'm gonna walk up ahead, Dad, I say, interrupting
him. I follow the curve of the tiny gravel path, lined
with scrub, past the metal shed to the ocean and the best
view of the bridge, where the water flows cold, even
from here.

Happy Days Motor Inn

It's check-out time and while he lowers her flowered suitcase and matching garment bag into the trunk she returns to their room to investigate, to see if they have left anything behind. Everything is here: coin-operated television set, framed mirror, tourist book in the third drawer. A punch cradled in the bathroom door. They can go now.

Back at the car, he tells her about the weird dream he had last night, the one about knifing a stranger, and the lack of blood at the scene. He asks her if she dreamt last night, but this time, she's the one who says she cannot remember. In his dream, she was there but not there. She was the one he killed, the one he saved.

From this angle in the parking lot, she can see the cleaning lady in Room 216, throwing linen into the middle of the floor. The bedspread piles up, shape of a crouching girl.

Deadpan

When another school
photograph broadcasts on Channel 9,
I know she's already gone. Something
about the picture's composition,
pink lipstick and white angora,
rich brown flop, a forbidden confection.
Her lazy eye, a far-off expression
already bracing against
what was to come.

Did our school's photographer see this
as well? With particles of chalkdust
reflected in his flash, glittering in descent
around her body, did he stop himself
from staring too long, from saying,
Smile?

Fertility Window

With a thwack on the sliding glass door,
Marjorie from two houses down, interrupts us.

Her baby has vanished.

My husband gets dressed,
searches with other men from the block.

I fix her a cup of coffee and she confides
she's pregnant again — and relieved
Because just in case and *what if
something happens?*

Troll

It's the shape of the three-year-old
that's off. The waistband of his black and white parka
bunched, bulky with building blocks. He waddles
to the rear of the daycare like an old skunk foraging,
and then, forgetting. His puffy sweat pants
smartly tucked into dark miniature cowboy boots.
With a grunt, he attempts to karate kick the door open.

Most days, Miss Cody resigns herself to shake him
down on arrival — the repeat offender trying to slip
across the border. This morning, she simply
points out the sign: TOYS FROM HOME
ARE FORBIDDEN AND WILL BE CONFISCATED. She adds
his blocks to a tub of trinkets behind her desk.

During free-time, the boy becomes
noticeably agitated playing house. The floor littered
with toy cans of vegetables he cannot
open, a carton of milk that contains no
liquid, four plastic eggs, uncrackable.

During the sing-a-long, he mouths
the words to *Kumbaya,* whacking himself
with the tambourine. At nap-time, he sleeps
but is difficult to wake. When the boy's mother arrives
to claim her son, she is charged
a late fee, much like when she forgets
to return a video.

Once safe at home, the boy swallows a doll.
A troll doll. The smallest
of dolls, its hair and eyes permanently petrified.

At the hospital, he motions
to the ultrasound screen, says, *Baby. Let me
hold my baby.* Then, wanting to please,
says, *Don't you dare come out!*

Manjeet

In a department store line-up a woman
in a sari clutches small green thongs.
Her daughter wanders the aisles, strokes packs
of gum: orange, fruit, melon, red. The display rack
squeaks, personalized toothbrushes, hairbrushes, barrettes.
ALISON, AMY, BARBARA, BRENDA. Names twirling
making the girl dizzy like somersaults onto blue mats,
names swirling like wooden whirligigs in the backyard,
spinning the rack, looking. CARLOTTA, CARMEL, CAROLYN.
A name. She shows her mom purple barrettes,
CHRISTINA etched in shiny yellow font,
like gold. She asks, *Can I have this?*

Blue Grandma

Betty McIntosh is called Blue Grandma by the entire McIntosh family. One morning, over thirty years ago, Stacey, the first grandchild, picked the bathroom lock, and witnessed Betty clasping up her satin blue brassiere. Hence, *Blue Grandma*. My goodness! Blue Grandma was never so embarrassed in her life. But now Blue Grandma is more concerned about the hairy beast that lives in her closet. Hairy Beast wears her clothes, including her dresses, and dirties them. His drool is so foul smelling that Blue Grandma is scolded for hiding food in her room. Stacey, now well into her forties, with children of her own, says, *Don't worry, Blue Grandma. There are no such things as monsters.*

Prayer for Her Future Husband

I want to tell you about eight things I've read lately and then I am going to go ahead and tell you a story like anybody else would.

1. *An eleven-year-old boy from the States hated his smell so much he saturated himself with Right Guard, day after day, month after month, until he collapsed one morning and died as a result.*

2. *The police shot at a car for speeding, killing the driver as he rushed to hospital to save his convulsing three-year-old daughter (who was saved).*

3. *A French woman was granted permission to marry her dead lover in Our Lady of Sorrows Catholic Church.*

4. *An old woman, riddled with lung cancer, wanted to give away her seaside bed-and-breakfast before she died . . . and then she changed her mind.*

5. *An amateur paleontologist in Nova Scotia just discovered the fossilized remains of a dog-sized beast that was never known to exist before.*

6. *A Brazilian farmer caged like a rabid dog for thirteen years by his wife and her lover was freed by his cousins yesterday.*

7. *Three weeks from now, a gargantuan 21-bit comet, called the Shoemaker-Levy 9, will smash into the planet Jupiter creating another moon for the sky.*

8. *Seventeen years ago an old man from East Vancouver buried his childhood tricycle in his front yard to ward off death.*

At forty-four, Starlie Severn looked like a little girl. Slim, flat-chested (even after breast feeding each one of her three babies to twenty months), and just under five feet, Starlie couldn't even glance sideways at a Cold Beer & Wine Store without being asked for identification. Usually when Starlie's husband Jake accompanied her, nobody would ask her age, but when they did ask, he was the one who was flattered, making a peeping noise like a small animal might. *She looks the same as the day I married her*, he'd tell the inquiring cocktail waitress or doorman.

And Starlie did look the same; Jake was no liar. Starlie still wore her long blonde hair off her face in a sweeping ponytail or clipped back with a long tortoise shell clasp. She still wore the same kind of clothes she wore in high school too. Tight blue jeans and white T-shirts. Simple white sneakers she would bleach every so often until they started to wear thin and she'd have to pick up a new pair at the department store. Casual stuff you'd wear to the market or slip on to mow the lawn or take out the trash.

Starlie could never get away with wearing what Jake wanted her to wear. Suits, dresses, high-heels, and nylons that wound themselves up tight in plastic eggs made her look like she'd borrowed someone else's clothing. Sometimes, dressed the way Jake wanted her, she looked like what her father used to call *Cheap.* It didn't matter much anyways, she had no need for fancy things, she hadn't worked since

Blane was born fifteen years ago. Then came Brittany, then Jake Jr..

Last summer when a wasp had stung the baby's eye, Jake and Starlie rushed Jake Jr. to the emergency and the on-call doctor referred to Jake as Starlie's father. Luckily, Jake didn't catch on, or maybe he chose to ignore the comment.

It was as though Starlie was trapped in a time warp or a wormhole or in a place outside of time. She should ask Blane about these kinds of things; he seemed so obsessed these days with space and dinosaurs. Perhaps, she thought, somewhere down the line, a wrong turn was made. And she surely wasn't going to grow up until she back-tracked and set things right. Starlie took a moment to inspect herself in the oval mirror above the fireplace. She was flawless. Not one wrinkle.

When Starlie reflected on her life (when she had a moment between the dust balls behind the fridge, tissues shrivelled in the kids' pockets, kitchen drawers cluttered with twist ties, take-out menus, empty tinfoil rolls, and burnt tea cozies), she couldn't find any misplaced steps. She did things by the book. She had met Jake in her senior year, fell in love with his red hair and his soft blond eyelashes that belonged to a kitten's face. He had a large space between his teeth that she thought would likely fill in but never did. Throughout their marriage, she grew to like his teeth just the way they were. After a glass of wine or two, she would pull Jake close and playfully lick the gap in his mouth.

She took her father's advice and completed college. She even waited a year before she allowed Jake to pop the question. *Are you planning on looking after my little girl?* her father asked Jake one evening after Sunday dinner. Jake nodded. Starlie's father poured him a scotch, *Come by my office Monday morning and I'll see what I can do for you.* Jake had worked for the business ever since and, in some ways, was now closer to Starlie's father than she was. When he called he'd always ask for Jake or one of the kids.

Then came the wedding. It wasn't the Catholic wedding Starlie and her father had always hoped for her. It was a Lutheran ceremony. *Close enough*, Starlie's father had said even though he once was an altar boy, *Close enough. As long as you have prayed to find the right young man. A man who will help you get into heaven, you can't go too far wrong.*

And Starlie had prayed for her future husband since her First Holy Communion. Prayed and prayed every night to Jesus to keep her future husband safe for she had fears that he might die even before they had met. When Starlie and her father travelled into town on the freeway, she had the feeling her future husband was out there, passing them or taking the next exit. Sometimes when Starlie prayed, she'd cozy up to her pillow, and smother herself with it, pressing her face down so hard she'd bolt up, panting. *Oh Jesus. Oh Jesus.* Other times, in the bath, Starlie would hold the shower massage against her belly and pray her future husband would be fertile and that he would bring her lots of children who looked like him.

Blane especially looked like Jake. Same colouring. Same big happy freckles that you want to find a secret code or pictures in. At fifteen, Blane also had Starlie's youthful look to him. It was too hard to see if the other two kids, Brittany and Jake Jr., had this trait as they were still under ten and, of course, they looked like children.

The kids had been non-stop talking about the junior lacrosse finals for weeks. Blane was hoping to try out next year. Brittany was already playing field hockey. Jake Jr. couldn't stand being left out. Starlie's father planned to take them to the game, then to Pizza Hut for all-you-can-eat. They'd be home by 8:30 or 9:00. Just enough time for Starlie and Jake to eat and do a few things by themselves without being interrupted.

After dinner, Starlie headed for the rec room. Jake always cleaned up after dinner. For the first years of their marriage, she'd try to help him clear the table or at least dry the cutlery but Jake would chase her out of the kitchen, whip her bottom with a damp tea towel. *Sit down, Your Highness*, he'd joke. When she insisted, Jake would be firm with her, *It helps me relax*. He wouldn't have anything to do with an automatic dishwasher either, even though Starlie's father had offered to buy them one last year for Christmas.

Curled up in her brown corduroy recliner, an afghan draped over her naturally hairless tiny legs, *Jeopardy* on mute, Starlie thought that Jake never wanted to give her any reason to complain. Maybe that's why she looked so odd, so much like one of Brittany's moon-faced plastic dolls, a lollipop, a big round head and a small stick body. The answer to *Final Jeopardy* was Munchausen's Syndrome and she knew the answer because she had read about it in the newspaper and heard about it on the late night national news.

She also knew about Munchausen's Syndrome by Proxy and that many children had suffered terrible ordeals. Usually it was the mothers who fabricated symptoms in their children, subjecting them to medical tests and surgical procedures. Starlie prayed for these mothers, *Oh Jesus, show them the way*, as she prayed for all her enemies.

I'll be upstairs, Sweetie, Jake said, striding up the carpeted stairs. He'd be on the computer all night, the white light of the computer screen bouncing across his face, making him look paler than usual.

Starlie fished for the Anne Tyler novel beneath the cushion but was getting a bit frustrated reading it. It seemed like all Tyler's heroines tried to escape their husbands, their families. Why wasn't anyone happy with their lot? She should talk, she thought. If she went on an adventure, if she just walked out their two-storey detached house, and never looked back, would she blossom into a woman? Would she wrinkle up, become who she was supposed to be, if her life was filled with tragedy, if Jake Jr. or Brittany had leukemia?

Just after nine, she heard her father and the kids pull into the driveway. She heard Jake stirring upstairs, the screech of the modem as he tried to reconnect the line. *Anybody home?* Jake Jr. said as he opened the door. Starlie laughed, of course they were, what was she thinking?

Look at you, little man, Starlie said, *skin a rabbit*. She pulled his dirty T-shirt up and over his head and smelled him. He smelled like pizza and outside. *Let's run you a tub. Where is everybody?*

Then Jake came downstairs and hugged his baby. Jake Jr. ran from his dad and giggled, trying to instigate a game of tag. Jake ignored him and put his arms around his wife. *I don't believe this*, he said, *you've got a grey hair. Your first.* Starlie looked at Jake. He had several grey hairs and a few on his chest. They kissed and she flicked her tongue inside his mouth and he smiled.

Mum, Dad. Come quick. Blane's digging up the front lawn! Brittany galloped back outside. Jake Jr. followed and screamed, *You're it.*

Starlie looked out the bay window in the living room, the Anne Tyler novel still in her hand, and parted the curtains just in time to see her would-be paleontologist son carefully brushing away the dust from what looked like the handlebars of a bike.

Accident

It's dark outside, heading home,
sixty clicks down the freeway, a fit
of police lights ahead, we decide to turn off,
take the long way. Our daughters, dormant
(finally) in the back seat, all trip preoccupied
with The Fives Game. They begin
with everything — five cities, five numbers, five
cars, five names — the potential to travel
anywhere, meet anyone. When the dice roll,
each sum strikes out possibility; our twelve-year-old now
destined to marry David, birth three children,
drive a Corvette to Jamaica. The baby of the family,
just turned eight, a childless widow, barely
scraping by in a loft in Tokyo.

And me, their mother, only yesterday in Barnes & Noble
intrigued by the teens crowded around *The Secret Language
of Relationships*, looking up birth dates, checking
compatibility. It doesn't surprise me —

we are meant to be with one another.

Entering our neighbourhood, the girls awake, an alarm of familiarity, slow car reaching home.

Lure

The first time I held
a book open and read from it
a crow landed
on the edge of the patio
and barked at me, *Caw. Caw.*

A golden seal on the book's cover
shot off a beam so that a small hole blazed
and smoked above the railing.

In the crow's beak,
the book, now airborne,
simply flapped out of sight.

Finally able to sleep, I fell
outwards, deep into the sun,
the sound of a brass-bound clock,
beating through old blankets.

Acknowledgements

Grateful acknowledgment is made to the editors of the following publications where these poems have appeared, sometimes in a slightly different form and/or with different titles.

"Probe" and "Imagine A Stranger" on-line at greenboathouse books;

"Horizontal Iceberg," "Jelly Fish Child," "Something Round," and "Terminology" on-line at Edgewise ElectroLit Centre;

"Troll" and "Prayer for Her Future Husband" in *Other Voices*;

"Shimmering Strip," "Even Outside", "Something Round," "Bird Land," "Luv Junket," "Taffy," "Chaos Theory," and "Running Amber" in *sub-TERRAIN*;

"Small Penis Poems," "Four of Everything," "Potato Peeler," and "Jelly Fish Child" in *Room of One's Own*;

"Pump Fish" in *Prism international*;

"Something Round," "Pump Fish," and "Jill Started Shaving" in *Breathing Fire: New Poets of Canada*. Edited by Lorna Crozier and Patrick Lane (Harbour Publishing, 1995);

"Manjeet" in *Contemporary Verse 2*;

"Super Socco Story," "Southern Accents," "Do You Want to Buy My Sister? She's Really Cheap," "Begging for Cookies," "Jean Fox & Debbie," "Little French Maid," "Children Who Look Like Ice Cream," "Clinking Glasses," "Pretend Mole," "Scotch Mints," and "Clichéd Super Socco Stories" in *Super Socco and Other Super Stories* (Ga Press; reprinted by Tiny Bat Books) and *Geist* as well as on-line at The Swiftsure Magazine;

"How do Snake Handlers Fall in Love?" and "Potato Peeler" in *The Lyre*;

"The Colour of Your Choice" in *The Capilano Review*.

Thanks

I would like to extend my love and gratitude to Andrew (my editor, husband, best friend), my parents Bud and Judy, who said I could be anything I wanted to be (including a Beautiful Dancing Lady), Glenys and Jim McEvoy, my sisters and their families, my teachers Jane Southwell Munro, Bill Kinsella, Dave Godfrey, Derk Wynand, Lorna Crozier, and my friends Diane Buffam, Diane Dewinetz, Samara Brock, and Ewan "F" Deane. Thanks also go to Brian and Anvil Press, the 7SWG, and to Alex and Carlotta and the gang at Airwaves Sound Design.

About the Author

Judy MacInnes Jr. was born in Prince George, British Columbia in 1970. Raised in Surrey, a graduate of Kwantlen College, the University of Victoria (B.F.A.), and the University of British Columbia (M.F.A.), Judy has worked as an administrator and researcher in the film industry since 1994. Her writing has been anthologized in *Breathing Fire: Canada's New Poets* (Harbour), *Eye Wuz Here: Women Writers Under Thirty* (Douglas & McIntyre), *Northwest Edge: Deviant Fictions* (two girls; forthcoming), *In the Trenches: The Best of sub-TERRAIN* (Anvil; forthcoming) and has appeared in a number of Canadian literary magazines. She is the author of the chapbook, *Super Socco and Other Super Stories* (Ga Press; reprinted by Tiny Bat Books). She lives in Vancouver with screenwriter Andrew McEvoy and their Norwegian Forest cat, Oscar.

Anvil Press publishes contemporary literary
titles in all genres.

Write for a free catalogue of books.

Anvil Press
#204-A 175 East Broadway
Vancouver, B.C. V5T 1W2
CANADA

T: (604) 876-8710

email: subter@portal.ca
www.anvilpress.com